AF262595

THE NATURE SERIES

For Irene & The Alchemist

SHELLS

**A GUIDE FOR
THE CURIOUS**

Susan E. Clark

Quadrille

PART ONE
ALL ABOUT SHELLS

PART TWO
SHELLS TO SEE

DECODING THE HIDDEN STORIES OF TIDE, TIME AND LIVES LIVED IN SECRET

Pick up a seashell and take the time to really look at it. What shape is it? What colour? How does the surface feel – rough or smooth?

Was this the home of a once-living creature that preferred to stay quiet and unnoticed, or one that boldly proclaimed: *I've arrived!*

Some shells, like the delicate cowrie, are as tiny as a thumbnail; others, like the conch, are large enough to blow into and call a ceremony into being. And despite their often-remarkable differences, every shell begins the same way – with the simple act of a soft, vulnerable creature building its own world, one layer at a time.

To pick up a shell is to touch both architecture and autobiography. It carries a hidden record of tides, of storms survived, of seasons of plenty and those more lean. Shells are part armour, part adornment, both a home and a history.

These are stories you can learn to decode – and that's what this *Curious Guide to Shells* is here to help you do.

Across the world, shells have been traded, worn, worshipped and worked into our own shelters. They are talismans and tools, jewellery and currency, myth and metaphor. They speak of journeys taken and transformations endured.

This book gathers the many lives of shells – as builders, as storytellers, as silent keepers of the sea's deep time – and offers them back to you, to hold, to marvel at, and perhaps to keep in your pocket as you walk home from the shore.

Welcome then, to the secret world of *conchology*: the study of seashells.

PART ONE
ALL ABOUT SHELLS

WHAT IS A SHELL?

A seashell is a skeleton, but one on the *outside* of an animal's body, which makes it an exoskeleton. Almost every shell you'll ever see, pick up or admire was made by a mollusc, a creature that has either died or been eaten, leaving its shell behind.

Shells themselves are not alive, but the creatures that once inhabited them were full of life and mystery: they had parents, habitat preferences, favourite foods, mating rituals and unique ways of moving through the world. We rarely pause to think of all that life inside the spiral.

All seashells are made primarily of calcium carbonate, which is the same substance found in eggshells and chalk. It's secreted by a soft tissue called the mantle, which lines the inner edge of the mollusc's body and builds the shell from the inside out – layer by layer, expanding and thickening as the animal grows.

You can think of a seashell as a portable home – a safe place to shelter from predators and other hazards. But it's more than just a dwelling – a shell is also a record of the animal's life: its curves, ribs and whorls are a living autobiography.

Holding a shell is like holding a memory, one that stretches back through the years. And if it's a fossilised shell in your hand, it might take you all the way back 550 million years, to the Ediacaran Period – before dinosaurs.

HOW SHELLS ARE MADE

The spirals, ridges and whorls you see on the outside of a shell are the tell-tale signs of how that shell was made by the sea creature that once lived inside.

The mollusc draws calcium from the surrounding seawater and converts it to calcium carbonate. The mantle then secretes this, along with proteins, onto the outer edge of the body, where the mixture calcifies and hardens to form a protective casing.

Imagine you're looking at a clam shell: the rounded nub at the narrowest point – the umbo – marks the birth of the shell. The widest part is the most recently formed section, and you can often trace growth lines across its surface, like tree rings in miniature, revealing how the shell expanded as its living inhabitant grew.

WHY ARE SHELLS SO BEAUTIFUL?

The beauty of some shells is much more than first meets the eye. Iridescence, for example, comes from microscopic structures in the shell layers that bend and refract light. Other colours arise from pigments the animal itself produces, for example, blues, violets, russets and golds:

The **green turban shell** (*Turbo marmoratus*) hides a lining of shimmering mother-of-pearl, its smooth spiral concealing a luminous sea-green heart.

The **map cowrie shell** (*Leporicypraea mappa*) is a study in elegance, with a polished surface traced in fine, map-like markings.

The **scaphella volute shell** (*Scaphella junonia*) – once so rare it became legendary among shell collectors – is patterned in rich, caramel blotches on a cream background, like a natural porcelain.

CLASSIFYING SHELLS

Scientists classify living things into groups to make them easier to study. Seashell-bearing animals mostly belong to the phylum **Mollusca**, which includes seven classes:

- **Bivalvia** (bivalves) – cockles, clams, scallops, mussels, oysters

- **Gastropoda** (gastropods) – snails, whelks, cowries

- **Cephalopoda** – nautiluses, octopuses, squids

- **Polyplacophora** – chitons

- **Scaphopoda** – tusk shells

- **Aplacophora** – worm-like molluscs which have no common names

- **Monoplacophora** – cap-like shells bearing one plate as seen with the deep-sea limpet

Most seashells you will find are in the first two groups.

BIVALVES

Scallop, oyster, mussel, clam, cockle

These animals have a two-part shell (hence 'bi' valves) joined by a hinge and closed by powerful adductor muscles. Scallops, for example, can clap their valves to swim. Bivalves are classic filter-feeders – siphons draw water across the gills for oxygen and food. Many bivalves use a muscular foot to burrow. The shell growth lines read like a tide diary.

Defence strategy: Bivalves clamp their valves shut and bury themselves.

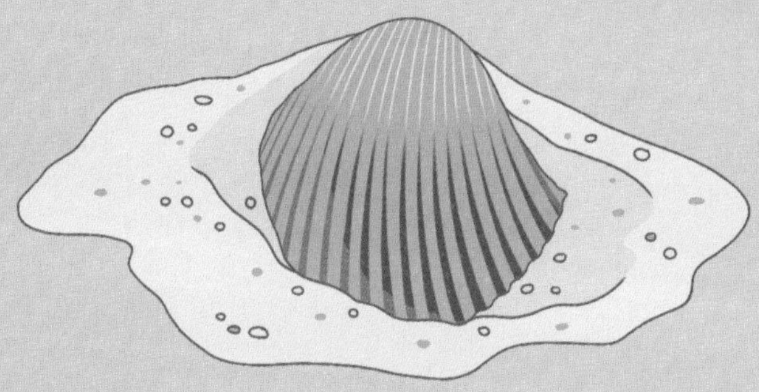

GASTROPODS

Cowrie, whelk, moon shell, auger, babylonia, turban shell

These creatures typically carry a single, often coiled shell. During growth they undergo torsion – the body twists so the mantle cavity and anus rotate over the head – a quirk with advantages for plumbing and defence. Movement is by a muscular foot. Feeding uses a 'radula', a rasping, tooth-studded tongue. Some gastropods have gills, others lungs, and a few have reduced – or lost – their shell entirely.

Defence strategy: Gastropods retreat and block the shell opening with an operculum (a trapdoor-like mechanism).

CEPHALOPODS

Nautilus, squid, cuttlefish, blue-ringed octopus

Cephalopods show just how spectacularly diverse molluscs really are. The nautilus lives in a multi-chambered house, steers with a jet of water, adjusts its own buoyancy and keeps its spiral external.

Squid and cuttlefish took a very different evolutionary direction and moved their shells inside. In squid, the 'inside shell' is more like a spine – a long, translucent chitin rod called the *gladius* or 'pen' that runs the length of the body. In cuttlefish, it's a porous aragonite cuttlebone, which acts as a built-in buoyancy aid. Internalising the shell makes these animals lighter, stiffer and far more manoeuvrable in water – in other words: super-fast.

The octopus let the shell go entirely, trading armour for compressible bodies, big nervous systems, and astonishing camouflage. Copper-based haemocyanin turns their blood blue. They have a parrot-like beak, a siphon for jet propulsion, and skin that blooms with colour from chromatophores.

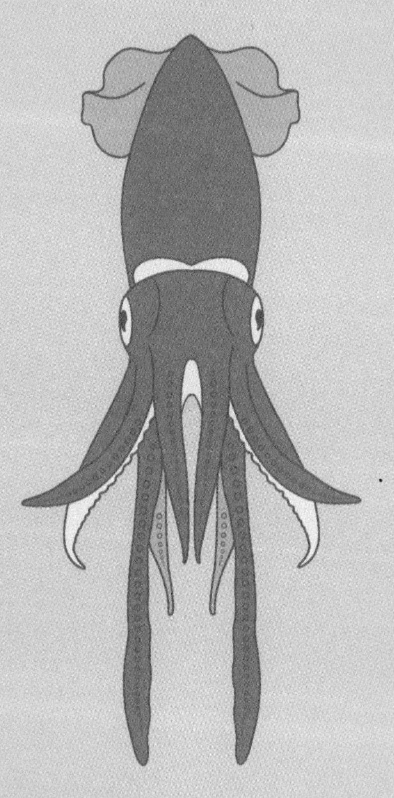

CHITONS

Gumboot chiton

Chitons took a different tack to cephalopods and developed eight overlapping armour plates ringed by a living girdle. They hug rock with a muscular foot and graze with a radula whose teeth are tipped with magnetite, turning them into iron-hard scrapers built for surf and storm.

Most species live in the intertidal zone, clinging so tightly they can survive the battering of waves and the probing of predators. Their shells can roll up slightly, like those of a woodlouse, to protect their softer underside. A fringe of sensory organs called *aesthetes* is embedded in the plates, allowing them to detect changes in light and shadow – some even have tiny image-forming eyes made of aragonite crystal.

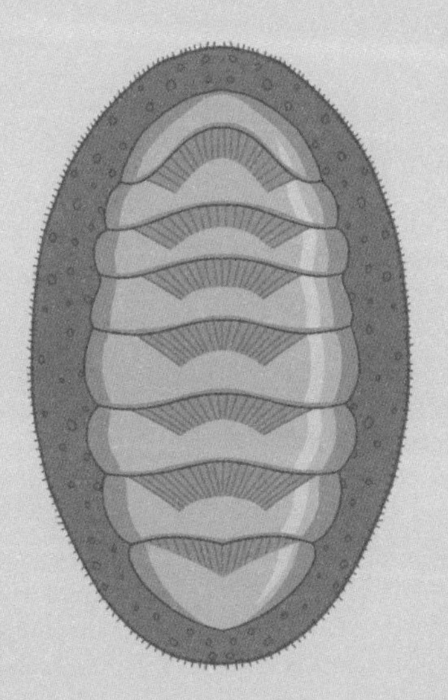

SPIRALS & SPINY BARRICADES

Nautilus, spiny murex, venus comb, thorny oyster, squid

Spirals are everywhere in the natural world. You'll find them in the swirl of a sunflower's seedhead, in the quiet geometry of a fir cone, and in shells ranging from the nautilus to the spiral conch.

Many shell spirals follow the celebrated Fibonacci spiral – a curve that expands in a steady, harmonious ratio, allowing the creature to grow without ever changing shape. The shell simply unfurls around its hidden axis, whorl by whorl, as if obeying an ancient script, written long before it was born. Each visible turn of the shell is a full 360-degree revolution.

Whorls are common in gastropods, and (for the fossil collectors among you) in ammonites, which are shelled cephalopods that died out about 66 million years ago.

Other species such as the thorny oyster, spiny murex and the fearsome venus comb, choose armour over spiralled elegance. Their spectacular spines jut from their shell, forming a defensive 'barricade', breaking up their outline and keeping predators at bay. Beauty here is barbed, with a clear warning writ large in calcium carbonate.

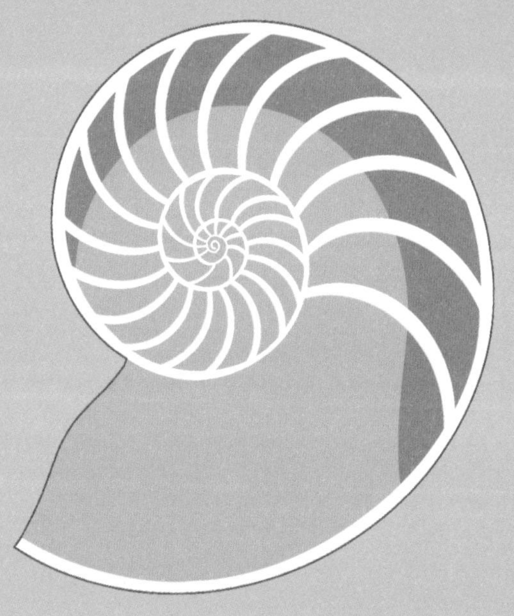

ANOMALIES & CURIOS

Carrier shell, keyhole limpet, paper nautilus

Not all shells follow the usual rules. Some are so light they seem to carry more air than substance, and others are so oddly-shaped they defy neat classification, reminding us that, in the shell world, as in life, there's always room for the unexpected. Here are three families in this special group:

• Carrier shell (*Xenophora*)
Some shells are architects; others are collectors. The carrier shell cements stones, coral and fragments of other shells to its own, turning itself into a travelling mosaic. Whether for camouflage or decoration, the result is part-armour, part-art – a portable gallery that grows as the animal does.

• Keyhole limpet (*Fissurella* – page 70)
This shell looks like a mini volcano with a neat little hole at the summit. That hole isn't damage – it's a built-in chimney for water flow.

• Paper nautilus (*Argonauta*)
Not a true nautilus but a delicate, paper-thin shell made by a female octopus as a brood chamber.

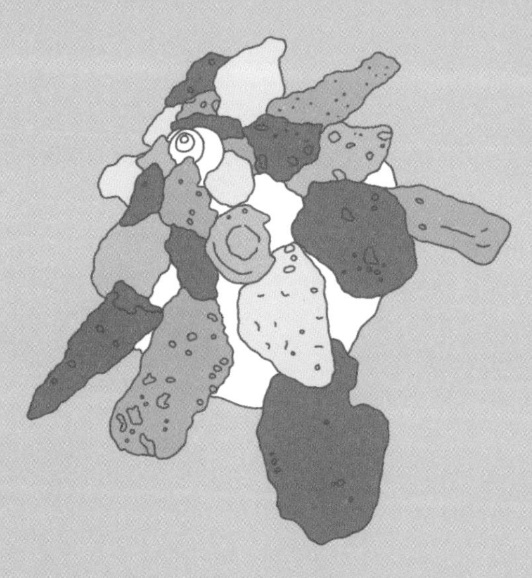

BORROWED SHELLS & VACANCY NOTICES

You might think a shell's story ends when its owner dies, but for some, that's just the first chapter, with much more to come. In the tide's shifting world, an empty shell is never wasted – it's a door left open for whoever needs it next.

Hermit crabs are the most famous creatures who like to move into other shells, often swapping shells as they grow. When several hermit crabs encounter an empty shell, they don't just fight for it – often, they'll form what's called a 'vacancy chain'. Here's what happens:

- The crabs gather near the new shell
- They line up from largest to smallest
- When the largest moves into the empty shell, its old shell becomes available for the next in line, and so on down the chain

It's an efficient beachside housing ladder, where everyone trades up in turn. Nobody is fighting for their piece of real estate; they're all happy to wait their turn.

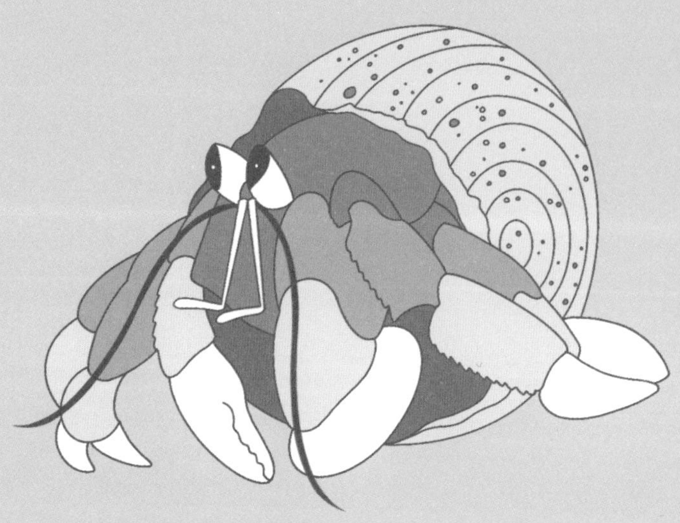

Some octopuses carry another creature's shell or some other hard structure for protection. The shells of another creature can act as a shield. The veined octopus (*Amphioctopus marginatus*) is called the 'coconut octopus' because it will tuck coconut halves under its arms and then use them to build a shelter. Small fish also shelter inside shells to hide from predators, and some coastal insects such as the common red ant (*Myrmica rubra*) will use vacant shells as part of their brood chambers laying their eggs under them and relying on the shells to trap heat.

CAMOUFLAGE & TRICKERY

'Now you see me, now you don't.'

Some sea creatures have mastered the art of disguise and deception, so while you think you've spotted something – well, you can't quite be sure. Some hide, and some pretend to be something else! Here are some of the ingenious ways shelled creatures practise deceit in plain sight.

Some shells appear to vanish the moment you glance away – the moon snail (*Polinices* spp.), for example, buries itself completely in sand leaving only a faint trail to hint at its presence.

Others, like the paper bubble shell (*Hydatina physis*), drift along the seabed wrapped in their own translucent mantle, making their outline hazy and hard to follow. Both use concealment as a way of living more safely in plain sight.

Others survive by looking like something utterly unremarkable. Cowries, with their high polish and rounded form, resemble wet pebbles at low tide. Nerites mirror the mottled greys and browns of the rocks they cling to. And some limpets flatten themselves so closely to adjacent barnacle clusters, the line between shell and neighbour disappears.

Camouflage isn't always about invisibility – sometimes it's misdirection. The scallop's row of vivid blue eyes, set along the shell's edge, can startle or confuse predators long enough for them to escape.

Other species use pattern to mimic warning colours, or to suggest movement where there is none, making an approach risky or bewildering – like the thorny oyster (*Spondylus varius*), whose jagged outline and bold red-and-white markings can resemble the spines and colours of venomous sea urchins.

Camouflage in shells is not cowardice; it's skill. It's the art of remaining unharmed in a world full of hungry mouths. Whether by vanishing into stone, masquerading as something inedible, or dazzling into confusion, these creatures prove that survival can be both clever and beautiful.

THE GLOW WITHIN

Inside some shells, a secret radiance awaits – layers of nacre, better known as mother-of-pearl, catching the light and throwing it back in shifting rainbows.

This stunning shimmer comes from structure, not pigment. Nacre is made of microscopic platelets of aragonite (a form of calcium carbonate) layered with elastic proteins. Light waves enter and bounce between these layers, interfering with each other to create the soft, rippling and eye-catching iridescence we see.

In the shell of the abalone (*Haliotis*), the colours can range from ocean green to deep violet, shifting with the angle of the light – like a wave turning over itself.

In warm tropical waters, the black-lip pearl oyster (*Pinctada margaritifera*) produces nacre with peacock greens and midnight blues, colours so deep they seem to contain whole oceans.

Pearl oysters use this same process to turn grit into treasure. When a tiny intruder slips inside the shell, the oyster coats it in layer upon layer of nacre, building a pearl as luminous as the shell's own interior – a slow, tidal architecture, built up grain by grain, until the surface gleams like moonlight.

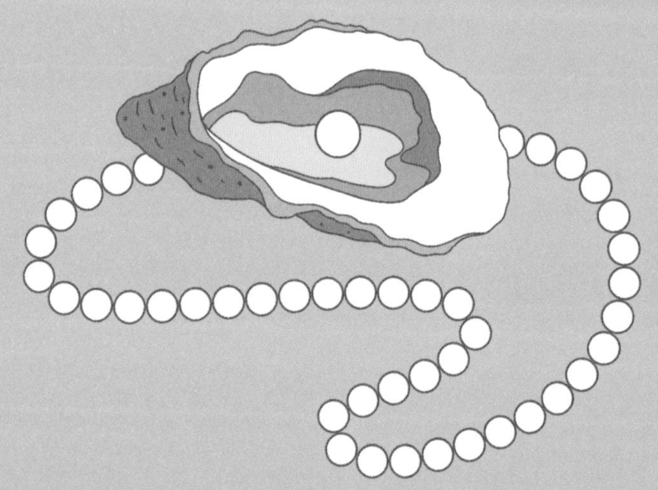

STRONG YET FRAGILE

The optical magic of shells evolved for strength as much as beauty.

Shell strength comes from layering. In species with nacre (mother-of-pearl), the inner layer is built from millions of tiny aragonite tiles stacked like bricks, held together with an elastic protein mortar. When hit, the tiles don't crack in a clean line, because the force of that impact has to zigzag, dissipating through countless micro-layers.

Other shells use different mineral arrangements, but the principle is the same: their layers are designed to deflect, blunt and absorb impact. This is why a clam can shrug off the powerful bite of a crab, that could snap a stick.

Seashells have much to teach us, and we are already learning from their inherent paradox: how something so seemingly fragile can also be remarkably strong – a lesson now shaping many fields, from architecture to space exploration.

In what is known as 'biomimicry', NASA (and others) have studied the intricate structures and processes found in nature – like those in shells – to push the boundaries of what's possible in technology.

Spacecraft shielding is inspired by research into nacre-inspired composites – by mimicking nacre's microstructure, engineers have created panels that are both lightweight and highly resistant to cracking – crucial for withstanding meteoroid impacts in space.

On Earth, architects are also turning to shells for inspiration. NASA's Orbit Pavilion is a giant, metal, seashell-shaped building where visitors can listen to the paths of the International Space Station and earth-orbiting satellites.

The Shell Lace Structure, developed by the London-based architects Tonkin Liu and widely adopted by architect Amanda Levete, draws directly from the ultra-thin, curving strength of natural shells. Using advanced modelling and fabrication, this approach produces lightweight but resilient forms that can flex without breaking, offering potential for buildings in earthquake or hurricane zones, as well as statement buildings to house art and other important cultural artefacts. A stunning example is the MAAT Museum in Lisbon – a beautiful modern building that unfolds like a scallop.

SHELLS FOR INSPIRATION

Once you know where to look, you'll start seeing shell-inspired structures in all sorts of unexpected places. If nothing else, 'spot the shells' is a fun game on day trips and holidays. You might notice shells in wall mosaics, in grottos, embedded in pathways, or in church and temple ornamentation.

In the UK, the crowning glory of the National Trust-owned A La Ronde house in Devon is its celebrated shell gallery – home to 25,000 shells.

In Spain, the Casa de las Conchas in Salamanca has a stunning façade studded with more than 300 carved stone scallop shells, each a symbol of the Order of Santiago and a nod to the city's place on the Camino de Santiago pilgrimage route (page 90).

Giant clam shells (*Tridacna gigas*) have been used as holy water fonts in churches. The church of Saint-Sulpice in Paris, for example, features two enormous clam shells gifted to King Francis I by the Republic of Venice in the 16th century. Clam shell fonts are also found in mission-era churches across Micronesia and Polynesia.

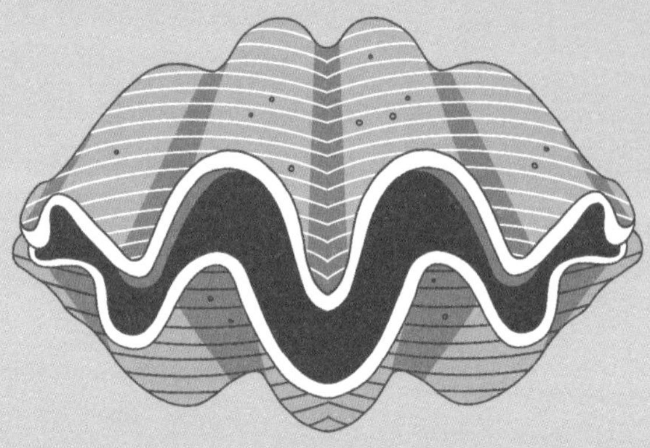

In Fiji, carved shell ornamentation appears on traditional *bures* (meeting houses), where the gleam of pearl shell is set into wooden panels as a sign of protection and welcome and in 17th to 19th century Europe, shell grottos, which had walls encrusted with thousands of shells in intricated patterns, were popular.

Shells are used as a symbol of rebirth, sanctuary and protection, yet also hold our stories – in trade, in treasure, and in the mythic symbols we carry across time.

SHELLS FOR CURRENCY & COLLECTING

Long before coins, banks and contactless payments, shells carried the kind of value we now call money. They were chosen for their durability, beauty and their limited supply. While shell money was never a single, universal currency, it was recognised across vast parts of Africa, Asia, the Americas and Australia as a trusted system of exchange.

The shells most widely used were cowries (*Cypraea moneta* and *Cypraea annulus*), both known as 'money cowries'. Their gleaming porcelain surface and distinctive shape made them easy to identify, hard to counterfeit and enduring in circulation.

Along the North American Pacific coast – from Alaska down to California – the most valued shells were tusk (*Dentalium*). Open at both ends, tusk shells could be strung on threads and traded by length rather than by number, with the highest denomination being a string about 15 cm (6 in) long.

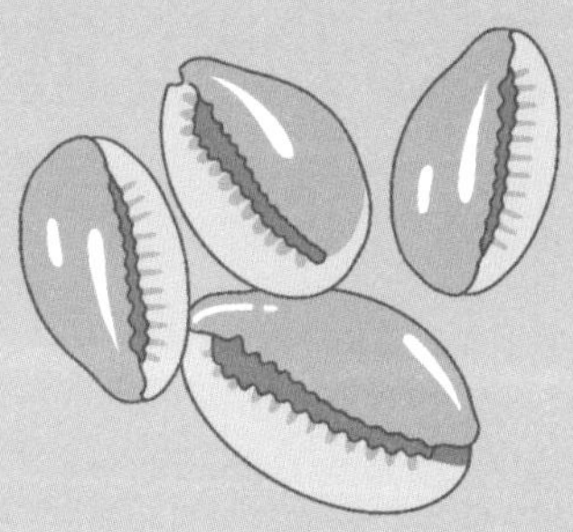

In Africa, shell money remained legal tender until as recently as the mid-19th century. In the Kingdom of Kongo, for example, the tiny, sparkling shells of the dwarf olive sea snail (*Olivella nana*) were used as currency, each carrying its own weight of trust in exchange.

But shells have never held only economic value; they are also tokens of admiration and affection, which is why so many of us keep a small collection on a windowsill or in a treasure box, each one carrying its own story.

For professional collectors, shells can command extraordinary sums. The large and striking *Conus gloriamaris,* once thought to be among the rarest shells in the world, can fetch hundreds of dollars. The value at auction depends not only on condition and rarity, but also on that old, familiar marketplace magic: who's in the room, and how fiercely they are bidding.

SHELLS AS ADORNMENT

Shells have long been used to make jewellery, decorate clothing and, in many cultures, as symbols of high status. Their natural polish, colour and intricate forms made them among the earliest materials humans chose to wear.

Across Oceania, cowries and other small shells are strung into necklaces, anklets and belts. Some wear cowries braided in their hair as a cultural statement of affinity with their ancestral lineage. In some island cultures, a finely worked shell ornament could signify rank or authority, passed down as heirloom and treasure.

In North America, tusk shells are sewn into clothing or worn as long strands that indicate prosperity and cultural belonging. For many Indigenous peoples, shell jewellery was – and remains – a way of honouring both lineage and the living land.

In Africa, cowries served a double role. They were currency, yes, but also embellishment, stitched into garments, crowns and ritual costumes. To wear them was to display your material wealth, and also invoke spiritual protection.

Shells also travelled far as trade goods, which meant that a necklace or headdress made of shells was not just beautiful, but a sign of connection to distant oceans. Adornment became biography: proof of journeys taken, or alliances forged.

Today, shells remain popular in jewellery and fashion. From the puka shell necklaces of the 1970s to contemporary designers adding them to a whole array of beach bags, hats and sandals, shells continue to carry their age-old associations of beauty and the sea itself – reminders that even the smallest fragment can become part of how we choose to announce our presence and be seen.

SHELLS & SOUND

Few childhood memories are more universal than that of holding a shell to the ear to 'hear' the sea. Pressed close, the shell seems to echo with the waves, a faint roar of the ocean, caught in its chambers.

In truth, what we hear is the sound of our own world amplified – air moving, blood rushing – yet the illusion remains enchanting. A shell becomes, perhaps, a way to hear the vastness of the ocean and a glimpse of our own vastness, too.

The sea-god Triton was said to carry a giant conch shell, which he blew like a trumpet to command the waves. In his hands the shell was an

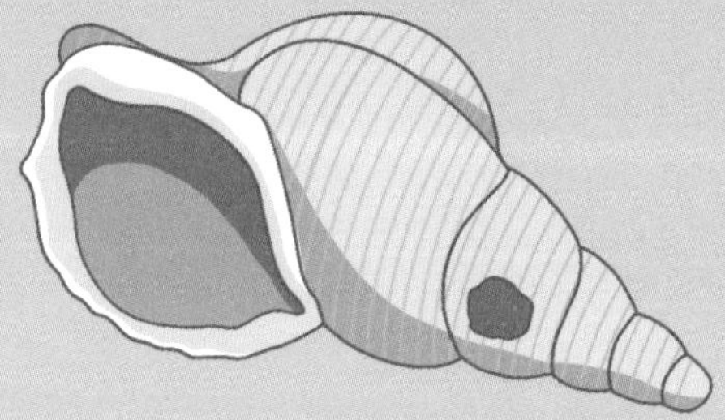

instrument of power – its spiral amplifying his breath into a call that could calm a storm or summon it. Conch shells have been used across the globe to call followers to scared ceremonies with its haunting sound.

This symbolism of sound in shells carries further. Their curves remind us that our own voices must travel through multiple chambers – lungs, throat and mouth – before it can be heard. So, shells remind us that we are resonant beings – containers of silence, vessels of sound. In every spiral is an invitation to listen, to speak, to sing.

MYTH & METAPHOR

Shells have always carried meanings beyond their surface. They are vessels of protection, symbols of beauty, and metaphors for growth and change. Whether heard, held or imagined, shells invite us to see both the natural world and ourselves in a new, perhaps more connected light.

We use the word 'shell' in everyday language as a powerful metaphor. We speak of someone 'coming out of their shell' or as having 'a hard shell'.

Shells resonate deeply as images of containment and protection, but also of revelation – a hidden beauty within. A shell can be a protective armour, isolating and defensive, or it can be a secure vessel, offering safety until the moment of readiness.

Aphrodite, the Greek goddess of love and pleasure, rose from the sea and was carried on a scallop shell, the seafoam of her birth gathering around her like a veil. Artists – including Botticelli with his famous *The Birth of Venus* – painted Aphrodite standing upon that curved stage, hair streaming, the shell both a cradle and a floating vessel of arrival.

And the spiral growth pattern of so many shells becomes the perfect metaphor for growth – each turn housing what has been and gone, each new chamber leading to what comes next.

In this way then, shells hold both the myth of arrival and the metaphor of becoming – carrying us all safely across life's many thresholds, both visible and invisible alike.

PART TWO
SHELLS TO SEE

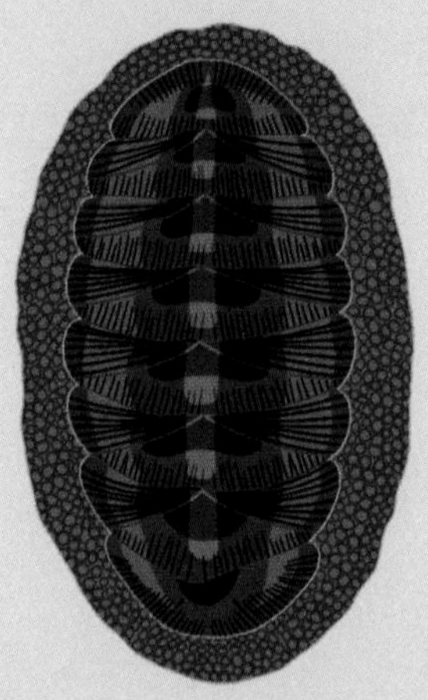

Also known as Angel or Butterfly Wings; put two of the shell 'plates' together, and you'll see why

ANGEL CHITON

Armoured marine mollusc · *Ischnochiton* spp.

Chitons – pronounced 'kite-ons' – are so old we have fossils of these marine invertebrates that date back at least 300 million years.

These ancient creatures live in tidal waters and their mottled grey shells offer excellent camouflage in their rocky homes. They live either singly, or in small groups of two or three, and are sometimes called 'suck rocks'; a clue about their behaviour.

The defining feature of these shells is the eight interlocking shell plates seen across their back, all of which are embedded in a tough, muscular girdle that surrounds the whole body. This is what is known as the 'dorsal' shell.

Super-strong, but also unexpectedly flexible, the chiton's protective shell can roll into a ball if threatened. Imagine a woodlouse curling into a ball – it's the same mechanism, one that is rare among sea creatures, but one that also allows the chiton to cling, with its foot, to an irregular surface.

When the chiton dies, the interlocking plates separate, and it's these parts you find as shells on the seashore. Some species show faint iridescence or mineral sheens, or become bleached to soft greys, pinks or greens when washed ashore.

The name chiton comes from the Greek word for tunic.

Found worldwide, from cold waters through to the tropics, and usually under rocks or in crevices.

Sometimes called 'coat-of-mail' shells – a reference to their carapace of eight interlocking plates, like the chain-mail armour of ancient knights.

The eight dorsal plates are made of aragonite – a mineral found in pearls.

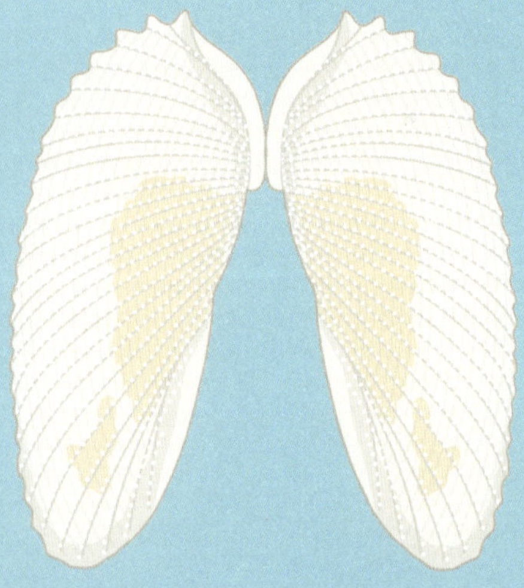

A sought-after shell with architectural radiance

ANGEL WING

Marine bivalve mollusc · *Cyrtopleura costata*

These bivalve molluscs burrow into rocks, woods, clay, mudstone and other hard surfaces to create long, cylindrical burrows. They secret an acidic substance to dissolve harder surfaces – including softer rock – and then use their powerful muscular 'foot' to pull themselves down to hidden safety.

These clams have a pair of siphons which are fused together to form a single structure, which reaches back up through the burrow to the seawater overhead. You can think of this structure like a 'snorkel': one siphon inhales water which is rich in oxygen and plankton, the other exhales filtered water and waste. This tube can be as long as 30 cm (11¾ in).

The name *Cyrtopleura* comes from Greek and roughly translates to mean 'curved side'. And while they may look delicate and ethereal, these shells are made of aragonite, which on the Mohs hardness scale, has a rating of 4, which is harder than a copper coin. That said, what makes these shells so highly prized is that it is rare to find the two angelic-looking wing halves still joined.

Found in the shallow coastal waters of the Northwest Atlantic.

These shells have a ghostly iridescence of lilac, pink or amber, thanks to the presence of minerals that catch the light.

Angel wings can grow up to 15 cm (6 in) long and will move at speed when threatened.

Their ability to stay buried and hidden is what keeps them safe in predator-rich coastal waters.

An understated beauty

ARCTIC COWRIE

Sea snail · *Trivia arctica*

The arctic cowrie is the northern (UK and US) cousin of the iconic tropical waters cowrie, which has been entangled with human culture for centuries (pages 40 and 42). This lesser-known version lives in sub-tidal waters, often hiding under rocks or seaweeds.

Look carefully for the arctic cowrie from April to October, tucked in among rocks and crevices – you might just find one hanging upside-down by its muscular, orange-coloured foot. The egg-shaped shell may be pale pink, buff, pale brown or even red, and you may see the fine antennae that it uses to sense the world around it.

When alive, this small sea snail wraps the whole of its shell in its mantle, covering it in a soft, brightly coloured living tissue that protects, repairs and rebuilds the shell. The mantle actively repairs tiny tears and rebuilds damaged parts using calcium carbonate, like a living lacquer.

When washed up on the beach, these little ridged, folded-over beauties are considered a real beachcomber's find!

Arctic cowries graze on sea squirts and bryozoans (simple invertebrates that live in sedentary sea floor colonies).

***Trivia arctica* sneakily lays its eggs in among sea squirt colonies – its favourite prey!**

This shell is much smaller than its tropical cousin, often less than 1 cm (½ in) long.

If you find a version of this shell with three dots on the top, it is likely the European 'cousin' *Trivia monacha*, sometimes called the spotted cowrie.

A strong Atlantic swimmer

ATLANTIC BAY SCALLOP

Marine bivalve mollusc · *Argopecten irradians*

This edible saltwater clam is a wondrous miracle of biology and survival. It's an hermaphrodite, meaning it has both male and female sex organs.

It also has 30-40 electric-blue eyes along the edges of its shell, giving it an otherworldly, even alien-like presence. While they appear to be along the edges of the shells, these unexpected eyes are embedded in the mantle – the frilly rim of soft tissue that you can see when the shell is open.

These eyes are not really like yours or mine; rather they are designed to detect light, shadow and motion so that the scallop can determine approaching threats, such as the looming shadow of would-be predators.

Each eye has a cornea and a lens, just like a human eye, but each eye also has a concave mirror made of plates comprised of guanine – one of the four main nucleobases that make up DNA. Here, it is layered in such a way that the plates catch and diffract the light to create the distinctive blue shimmer.

The Atlantic bay scallop is found mainly in the Northwest Atlantic ocean, and is a very strong and fast swimmer when provoked. It 'swims' by rapidly clapping its two shells together.

These bivalve scallops have thin, lightweight but strong shells that open and close at a hinge.

You can find these shells in a variety of colours, from brown, grey and black, to red, orange and yellow.

Atlantic bay scallops can grow up to 9 cm (3½ in).

The lifespan of the Atlantic bay is 12–26 months.

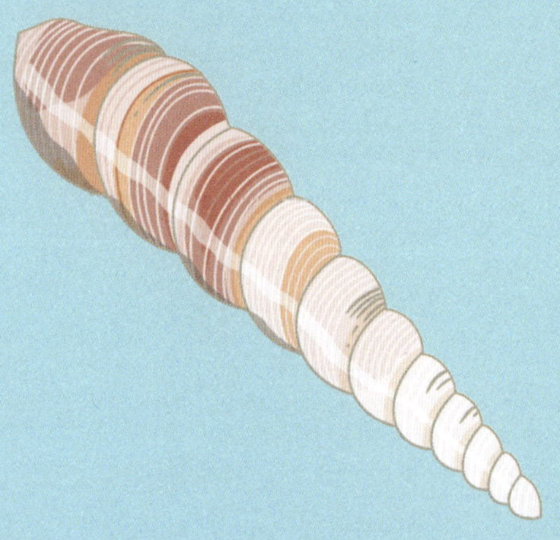

Can stun unsuspecting prey using venom

AUGER SHELL

Sea snail · *Terebra maculata*

Augers are sea snails and the *Terebra maculata,* which favours tropical waters, is one of those gorgeous shells you might bring back from an overseas holiday. If you find something similar on a UK or US coastline, you'll be looking at a smaller, but related, family member.

Shaped with an ingenious spiral 'drill', this is a 'boring' creature (meaning it drills downwards, not sends you to sleep in seconds). This is also a creature where the beauty of the shell may be a cover for a darker tale – the *Terebra maculata* are equipped with a harpoon-like 'tooth' and a siphon to detect and immobilise prey, using a venomous secretion. The 'tooth' is connected to a venom gland which delivers neurotoxins to stun its prey, usually small marine worms or other tiny invertebrates.

By the time you pick up the empty shell, this skullduggery is long gone. If you do come across a live specimen, don't worry – the venom is not strong enough to harm humans.

This family of sea snails were first named by Carl Linneaus in 1758.

The name, *Terebra,* comes from Latin and means to bore or drill.

These shells are typically long and slender, with 15–25 visible whorls.

With colours ranging from pale cream to rich caramel, often streaked or banded, these shells are prized for their symmetry, and will polish beautifully.

A scavenger with a taste for other snails

BABYLONIAN WHELK

Sea snail · *Babylonia areolata*

If you find a shell that looks as if it was carefully hand-painted with the markings of a giraffe, then you have stumbled upon a Babylonian whelk. Thick, glossy and popular with jewellery makers, thanks to its gorgeous and distinctive patterning, this is a conical, plump and rounded shell, adorned with brown spots or swirls on a cream or white background.

Babylonian whelks live in shallow sandy or muddy waters, preferring coarse-grained sand. They can grow up to 5 cm (2 in) in length and are carnivorous scavengers, known for feeding on sea urchins, scallops, marine worms and other sea snails. They can break the shells of their prey to access the nutrition-rich meaty insides. Researchers have even found tell-tale fragments of larger sea creatures, in their stomachs, including oysters, clams, squid and shrimp.

These whelks are night-feeders, burrowing in the sand to hide during the day, and emerging at night to hunt and feed by stealth and moonlight.

This is a large and diverse family (Buccinidae) with over 400 different species.

Babylonian whelks can live in both cold waters and tropical seas.

Whelks are farmed for food across Southeast Asia, especially China and Vietnam, where they are considered a delicacy.

In 2024, researchers completed the full genome map of *Babylonia areolata*, making it one of the most comprehensively studied gastropods to date.

A heart-shaped shell, steeped in folklore and music

COMMON COCKLE

Marine bivalve mollusc · *Cerastoderma edule*

When together, the two halves of a cockle shell form the shape of a heart, which is why there is the saying, 'It warms the cockles of my heart'.

This edible saltwater clam has also made its way into folk song. You might have heard the Irish ballad, *Molly Malone*, with its catchy refrain, '*Crying cockles and mussels, alive alive oh!*'

These sturdy, ridged shells protect a medium-sized clam that lives on muddy and sandy shores, between the high- and low-tide mark. It can grow up to 5 cm (2 in), but is usually smaller, around 2 cm (¾ in). Those you find washed up on the beach are usually off-white or yellowish on the outside, with a white interior.

As with many humans, cockles prefer to live in communities – just like an underwater village. They like to stay buried for protection, but only to a depth of about 5 cm (2 in). Common predators include shore birds, such as oystercatchers, as well as crabs and even some fish.

Commonly found along estuary tidelines in the UK, cockles are a food source for birds, fish and people.

Cockle shells are rounded and domed, with radiating ridges.

The cockle is a filter-feeder, using two retractable siphons – one to draw in seawater and filter plankton, and the other to eliminate waste.

These creatures reproduce by broadcast spawning, releasing eggs and sperm into the water at the same time.

A quiet species with a sinister secret

DOG WHELK

Sea snail · *Nucella lapillus*

Shall we get the sinister side of this sea snail out of the way first? At first glance, it may look pretty harmless, but the dog whelk is a voracious carnivore and will drill a hole in the shells of other sea creatures – such as barnacles and mussels – to suck out the meat of the creature inside.

To eat, the dog whelk uses its radula, lined with rows of tiny, sharp teeth. This, together with the secretion of a chemical substance designed to dissolve the shell of its prey, make the dog whelk a lethal killing machine.

These conical-shaped shells are usually white but may be grey, brown or yellow, and may have brown spiral bands. They grow to about 3 w (1¼ in) in height and end in a short, pointed spiral. You will probably find specimens with a hole in the spiral tip, which tells of murder-most-foul – in other words, another predator has eaten the whelk.

As well as preventing other species from taking over the seashore, dog whelks are an important pollution-indicator species. In the late 20th century, populations crashed after a chemical called tributylin (TBT), used in paint, leached into tidal zones causing the female dog whelks to grow male sex organs. Thankfully, that chemical is now banned.

Found from the Arctic to the Algarve, and common on the rocky coasts of the UK and Ireland.

Like limpets, dog whelks have a strong homing instinct and will return to the same spot between tides.

The egg capsules are shaped like vases and stick to crevices and overhangs in intertidal zones.

Dog whelks hide another gruesome secret – inside the eggs, where hundreds of tiny embryos develop, the strongest youngsters will often eat their siblings.

The strong, silent type

HARD CLAM

Marine bivalve mollusc · *Mercenaria mercenaria*

If a picture paints a thousand words, then a clam shell tells the story of time passing – slowly and quietly. The concentric growth rings, etched into these sturdy shells, offer some idea of the age of the clam: many clams live for more than five years, with each ring marking another season survived.

The outside of this shell ranges from dirty white to (let's be honest) filthy brown in colour. But that is just the outside, because look more closely at the inside and you will see just why the First Peoples living along America's Eastern Seaboard crafted decorative and ceremonial beads from these clams – and also used them as currency. Inside, the shell reveals a beautifully smooth, curved surface of creamy white tinged with a deep purple blush, a colour that intensifies near the hinge. It is this inner richness that gives these shells their quiet beauty.

Also known as the Northern Quahog, this is a large clam that can grow up to 15 cm (6 in). It lives in sandy, muddy intertidal zones and you'll need to dig down to a depth of at least 10 cm (4 in) to find one. Like so many marine creatures that stay buried for safety, it accesses nutrients and eliminates waste through a siphon – a hollow tube that reaches up from the sediment into the surrounding water.

This is an important commercial shellfish, although repeated attempts to farm it in British waters have been mostly unsuccessful.

The smaller the clam, the higher its value as a seafood delicacy.

Clams grow fastest at water temperatures of 18–25°C. Below 5°C, they become dormant.

The two sexes are separate, so eggs and sperm are released into the water for external fertilisation.

Handle with care for a coastline chorus

JINGLE SHELL

Marine bivalve mollusc · *Anomia simplex*

When dried and hung, a collection of these beautiful shells will jingle, sounding just like a wind chime or the clinking of sea-glass bells. That said, they have many other names too, including gold shell and, perhaps less appealing, mermaid's toenails!

Paper-thin, iridescent and translucent, the jingle shell is much stronger than it looks. It needs to be strong to withstand the environmental pressures of its chosen lifestyle because, rather than clinging to a rock or any other immobile surface, it hangs by a thread (literally) to other sea creatures, including mussels and barnacles.

This adaptation means the jingle shell can survive in the turbulent waters of coastal bays and estuaries, where the waves can be strong and the water is in constant motion. And so, by being cleverly anchored to another creature that can also move, the jingle shell is responsive to these changes.

These pretty shells are used in many industrial processes including the making of glue, chalk, paint and other materials.

Commonly found in the shallow waters of the Atlantic coast of North America.

Jingle shells come in a range of glorious hues from gold to lavender, coppery orange to pearly white.

Jingle shells are made from aragonite (a rare, crystal form of calcium carbonate), giving them their shimmering, almost glass-like appearance.

Look for these shells glinting in piles of tidal seaweeds.

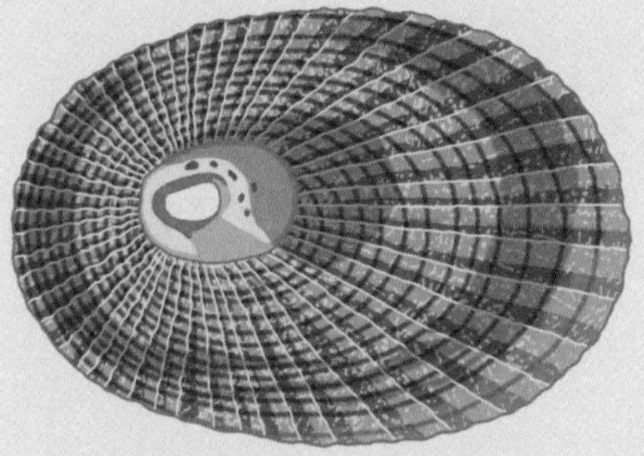

**Shaped like a volcano

KEYHOLE LIMPET

Rock-dwelling sea snail · *Diodora* spp.

These shells are easy to identify thanks to the volcano shape, with a keyhole at the top. The hole allows for the release of water and waste products, after seawater has been drawn in at the front of the limpet's body, passing over the gills.

Reproduction is external, synchronised and still something of a mystery. The males and females somehow know to release eggs and sperm into the water at the same time to maximise the chances of fertilisation. Science suggests this may be influenced by tides, temperature and moon cycles, but truthfully, it is a mechanism we don't yet fully understand.

Like so many sea snails, this limpet has a radula - a rasping tongue covered in tiny, sharp teeth which it uses to scrape sea sponges off the rocks. This tongue is reported to be the world's strongest biological structure!

Colours vary widely, so you may find white, grey, yellow, orange or even red keyhole limpet shells, which are often marked with radiating bands of brown or green.

Look for a conical, oval-shaped shell with a clear hole at the top.

These limpets are grazers, feeding on sponges and other detritus.

The keyhole limpet can grow up to 4 cm (1½ in), although most specimens are around 2 cm (¾ in).

Favourite habitats worldwide are rocky shores and the seabed itself.

Speed, size and stealth make for a successful seabed hunter

LETTERED OLIVE

Sea snail · *Oliva sayana*

Polished, smooth and shiny with purple zig-zag bands said to resemble Egyptian hieroglyphs – hence 'lettered'.

These large sea snails were first documented in 1834 after being discovered by Charleston physician and conchologist Dr Edmund Ravenel. Ravenel built a famous collection of shells from the waters and wetlands of South Carolina's coastal Lowcountry, publishing a shell catalogue that included the lettered olive.

Long before that, these beautiful shells were used by the First Peoples to create necklaces. They were also strung together to make *portiéres* (door-curtains) to sell to tourists.

Lettered olives have a cylindrical shell with a short spire and a long, narrow aperture that extends the length of the shell. The highly prized polished look is a result of the mantle wrapping around the whole shell to protect it.

When alive, the snail can retract its soft brown or purplish body back into the shell, sealing the opening with a tight-fitting operculum (a trap-door mechanism).

On May 8, 1984, the lettered olive was named the state seashell of South Carolina.

Most specimens are about 6 cm (2¼ in) long, although some have been recorded as long as 9 cm (3½ in).

These snails are fast-movers, using their large, muscular foot to power along.

The lettered olive is a voracious carnivore, devouring small bivalves and other molluscs, typically hunting at night.

Sometimes hanging on is the best survival strategy!

LIMPET

Rock-dwelling sea snail · *Patella vulgate*

If you go rock-pooling at the beach and the tide is still out, you might spot a limpet clinging on to the rocks. The limpet might look disinterested in its surroundings, but do not be fooled, because as soon as the tidal water washes back in, the limpet will be on the move, scavenging for algae.

As the tide heads back out again, this clever sea snail will return to the same, favourite, spot following a trail of mucus it left as a guiding pathway back to safety. Over time, the edge of the limpet shell wears away the rock at this favoured spot, to create a 'welcome home scar'.

There are many varieties of limpet native to British shores. The common limpet has a small, greyish conical shell. You may also find the black-footed limpet, with a smaller, flatter shell or a China limpet, with an orange patch on the inside of its shell.

If you are exploring among the rock pools at low tide, make sure to leave everything undisturbed and exactly as you found it, so the limpets can return home. A rock pool is an ecosystem in its own right – everything with a place of its own – and, as the limpet teaches us, with good reason for being in that specific place.

A limpet's grip is truly legendary – clinging to a rock, it can withstand up to 80 lb of force and resist crashing waves.

The limpet's strong muscular foot not only grips, it also contracts and can lock this sea snail in place for days on end.

The teeth that line the raspy radula tongue are made from goethite, an iron-rich material that is stronger than spider silk.

This sea creature favours intertidal zones and will travel over a metre to a favourite food source.

Delicate name, lethal stalker by nature …

MOON SHELL

Sea snail · *Neverita duplicata*

The moon shell leads a solitary life spent mostly burrowed under the sand. Every so often, its beautiful, discarded shell will be the only visible clue that it ever passed this way.

The female lays her eggs in a half-moon shape, known as an 'egg collar', which you might, at first glance, think is a bit of old rubber or plastic littering the beach. Inside, protected by a thick layer of slime and mucus, are up to 100,000, as yet unborn, baby snails. In water, this structure becomes rubbery and covered with sand, which provides another protective layer while the young hatch and grow.

Also known as a 'shark eye' snail, this deceptive creature is found in the Western Atlantic. It is a 'globular predator', which means its body is shaped like a globe, and will catch its prey by ambushing and enveloping it. It will then bore a hole into the protective shell of its prey, paralyse it with lethal chemicals, and then liquidise it for lunch.

Gruesome yes – but for collectors, this means the shells of that prey have a pre-drilled hole which is handy for stringing necklaces or windchimes!

Moon shells are sometimes called 'driller killers' because of the tell-tale holes they leave in the shells of their prey.

This snail is a nocturnal hunter, staying buried and out-of-sight by day.

Although solitary, moon shell populations can boom in a rich prey habitats, leading to the devastation of, for example, an entire clam bed.

The moon shell has some pretty unsavoury cannibalistic tendencies and is not averse to eating its own …

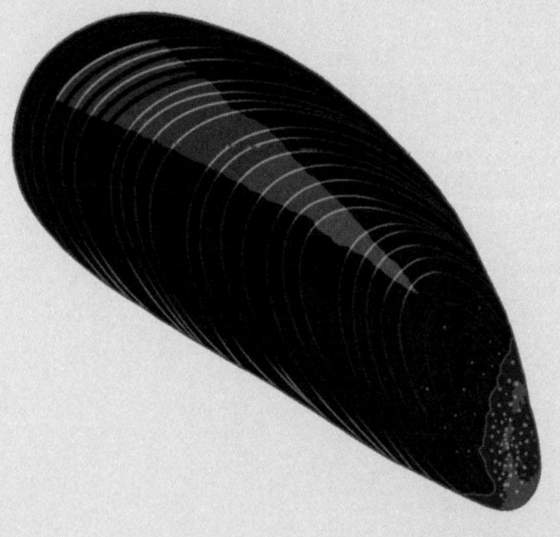

No mussel is an island

MUSSEL

Marine bivalve mollusc · *Mytilus edulis*

The common blue mussel – the one you see on the menu at seafood restaurants – is a familiar sight on shores all around the UK and the US. It is also a sea creature that quietly reminds us of family and community values.

These mussels form large, dense 'mussel beds' (communities) by attaching themselves to the sea floor and each other. They do this using sticky fibres called 'byssus threads' which are fine, silky filaments that they spin from their own bodies.

These strong bonds help the mussels withstand powerful tides and waves, and bind the community together for safety. Some mussel species use the threads to pinion a would-be predator, to fully immobilise it and stop it from eating or escaping.

The mussel bed itself acts like a miniature reef system – one which, when exposed by low tide, becomes an 'eat-all-you-can' seaside buffet for seabirds, especially oystercatchers.

Favoured habitats are rocky, sandy or muddy shorelines.

Mussels are a favourite food of people, birds, crabs, dog whelks and starfish.

Mussels are excellent filter-feeders, cleaning the water as they go. While often overlooked, they are important environmental heroes – quietly stabilising their ecosystems.

These molluscs will grow to between 3 cm and 10 cm (1¼ in and 4 in), and while the average lifespan is 2–3 years, they may live up to 10 years.

To touch this shell is to touch ancient time itself

NAUTILUS

Cephalopod · *Nautilus pompilius*

Kin to octopus, squid and cuttlefish, nautilus is the most ancient of all our featured shells – a sea creature which, according to fossil records, has remained virtually unchanged for 500 million years.

Writers, artists and engineers have long marvelled at this cephalopod's beauty, and also the graceful way it swims using jet propulsion, to 'pulse' through the waters of the deep ocean.

The soft-bodied nautilus lives inside a hard, coiled shell made of multiple connecting chambers. The creature itself occupies the outermost, largest chamber, using the others to regulate its buoyancy. The chambers behind are connected by siphuncle tissue (pronounced *sigh-funk-el*), working as a living canal, allowing the Nautilus to adjust buoyancy, up or down, with precision. Marine biologists call this a water column.

Sadly, these remarkable creatures are often caught for their beautiful shells, which are used in jewellery. Although there are currently no formal protections in place, nautilus populations appear to be in decline. This is a specimen best admired from photographs.

Living in the deep Indo-Pacific Ocean, the nautilus has up to 90 small tentacles.

The nautilus has a simple eye, more like a pin-hole camera, than the complex eye of an octopus.

Nautilus is often harvested for the shell's inner layer – the nacre, or mother-of-pearl – which is used as a pearl substitute in jewellery and ornaments.

In local culture, the nautilus is seen as a symbol of growth, regeneration and adaptability.

Gender-fluid and quietly extraordinary

OYSTER

Saltwater bivalve mollusc · *Ostreidae* spp.

Prized as a seafood delicacy with (unproven) aphrodisiacal properties, oysters are sea creatures in their own right, and a species that has been around for at least 15 million years.

For starters, an oyster left in its own habitat can live as long as 20 years. Throughout that life, an oyster may change sex – from male to female and back again – multiple times. The biological term for this is 'sequential hermaphroditism'. Most oysters start out as males because it takes less energy to produce sperm. Then, as they mature and become larger, they may become egg-producing females, able to harness the extra energy needed to produce eggs and release them into the water.

This flexible gender cycle enables an oyster colony to maintain a reproductive balance, a quiet, but extraordinary, biological wisdom that responds to the needs of the whole oyster bed, not just the individual.

And of course, we cannot talk about oysters without talking about pearls. Not all oysters produce them – pearl oysters belong to the *Pteriidae* family.

A grain of grit enters the shell. And instead of resisting it, an oyster wraps it, layer by layer, until what started out as discomfort and 'other' becomes luminescence. A magical alchemy, and a lesson for life?

Oysters are vegetarian filter feeders, consuming plankton and other organic matter from seawater.

Found in coastal waters and estuaries, oysters live in oyster bed communities which, in turn, support diverse marine life.

Oyster beds improve water quality, with adult oysters able to filter up to 50 gallons of water a day.

An oyster becomes an adult when it turns one-year-old. Juvenile oysters are called spat.

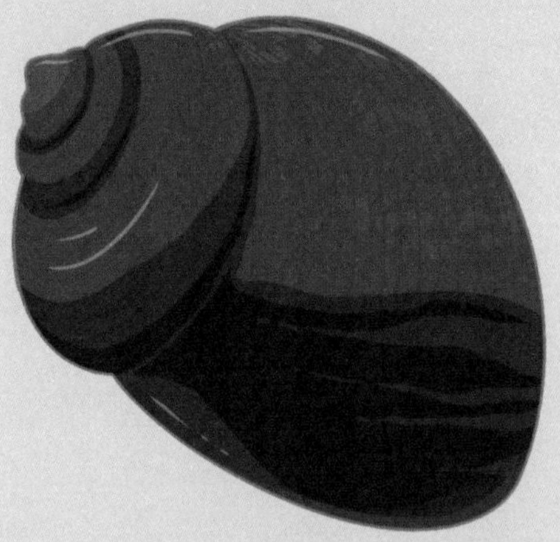

A clever little hitchhiker

PERIWINKLE

Large sea snail · *Littorina littorea*

This unobtrusive sea creature may not, at first glance, set your heart aflutter. However, being 'common' doesn't mean it's not special, but rather that it has something clever that's helped it to thrive

You can see large numbers of these sea snails – which look a lot like land snails – when you go rock pooling. Look carefully in cracks and crevices and chances are you'll see a group of them clumped together, quietly waiting for the tide to return.

One extraordinary thing about these snails is that, unlike others, with eyes on the tips of their tentacles, the periwinkle has eyes at its base. This means they 'feel' and sense their way with their tentacles, while their vision stays trained on the sea floor.

Part of their quiet genius lies in the fact that periwinkles can survive out of water for several days. Thanks to the presence of a modified gill that functions as a lung, the periwinkle can breathe at low tide, a clever adaptation that increases its chances of survival.

Native to Europe, these sea snails were introduced to North America in the 1800s, likely via the ballast water on ships. Today, they have become one of the best-known intertidal species along the eastern coastline of the US.

Found on rocks and among seaweed, usually at the lower- to mid-shoreline.

The shells are round, whorled and greyish-brown with concentric ridges and a pointed apex.

The shells always coil in a right-handed spiral so you will never find a left-handed periwinkle.

Also known as edible periwinkles or just winkles, these creatures are a popular seaside snack in the UK, served with vinegar and white pepper.

Iconic queen of the shells

QUEEN CONCH

Large sea snail · *Aliger gigas*

Think back to the very first time someone said, 'Here, listen – can you hear the sea?' The chances are, it was the iconic, pink-lipped, spiralled queen conch they placed in your hands.

This is the shell of childhood, fairytales and folklore, and it is also the home of a large sea snail that lives in the warm, shallow waters of the Gulf of Mexico and the Caribbean.

Queen conch may be one of the most iconic and easily recognisable shells in the world, but this species is now under serious threat, due to overharvesting for both the shell and its meat. In 2024, NOAA Fisheries – the national US body that protects ocean ecosystems – listed the queen conch as threatened under the Endangered Species Act.

So, don't be tempted to buy one of these for your collection, and inadvertently support its harvesting. Instead, you can simply admire it from the illustration here.

Although a herbivore, the snail, with its shell, can grow up to 30 cm (11¾ in) long and can weigh about 2 kg (4½ lbs).

This snail moves using a muscular foot and an operculum, which acts as a lever to propel the snail forwards in a 'hopping' gait.

The operculum also helps with defence – when the snail pulls back into the shell, it closes the doorway behind it.

The queen conch has a long history of sacred ceremonial use (page 45).

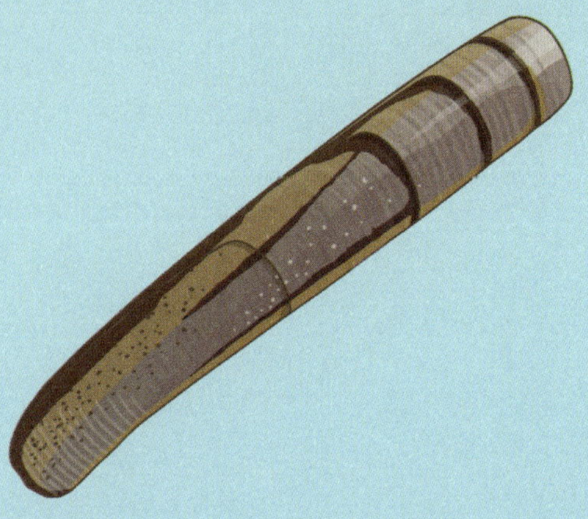

The 'Scarlet Pimpernel' of shells – a rare and precious find

RAZOR

Marine bivalve mollusc · *Ensis* spp.

The long, thin and slightly curved shell of the razor is named after the cut-throat razor blade, still used for shaving by traditional barbers.

The living razor lies buried and upright in the sand – a vertical 'blade' that can disappear in seconds when threatened, using its powerful foot to dig down, out of sight.

This configuration – head up, foot down – is simply extraordinary. It means the razor exposes very little of itself to a predator-filled world. All we might spot is the fine edge of one tip, which contains its feeding and breathing siphon.

This siphon also assists with the razor's rapid retreat: when danger strikes it can pump water up and out through this tube to loosen the sand overhead, clearing a path for its astonishing disappearing act.

In the UK, species like *Ensis ensis* and *Ensis siliqua* are common. Along the Atlantic coast of North America, *Ensis directus* – or the Atlantic jackknife clam – dominates.

Razor clam can burrow at a rate of about 1 cm (½ in) per second.

Often broken by the time they wash up on shore, these shells shimmer pale brown, green or cream. The shimmer is thanks to the iridescent inner lining.

Razor shells will be between 10 cm and 15 cm (4 in and 6 in) long.

Another common name is the jackknife clam.

A shell for guidance and spiritual devotion

SCALLOP

Marine bivalve mollusc · *Pecten* spp.

One of the most iconic shell shapes in the world, the scallop has long-held a symbolic resonance for humankind.

The large, fan-shaped shell of the great scallop (*Pecten maximus*) is found along British and North American Atlantic coastlines.

The smaller and more symbolic *Pecten jacobaeus* is the sacred emblem of the Camino de Santiago, and worn by pilgrims as a sign of faith and endurance. Historically, pilgrims walking to Santiago de Compostela were gifted a scallop shell upon completing the journey. The shell's radiating lines are said to represent the many paths taken by pilgrims. Scallop shells were also used to scoop water from rivers and springs along the way, making the shell both sacred and practical.

What most people recognise as a 'scallop' when served as food is the mollusc's adductor muscle – the thick, fibrous tissue the scallop uses to clap its two valves together, propelling itself forward in quick, purposeful bursts. This is one of the few bivalves that can swim.

Scallops cannot fully close their shell so they prefer deeper, cooler waters where fewer predators lurk.

The scallop has multiple eyes at the base of its tentacles and around the edge of its mantle to detect movement.

Scallop shells are usually tinged with cream, coral or amber – each one shaded by tide and time.

The scallop shape inspired the design of the Michelin Guide symbol for high class restaurants.

Gender-fluidity taken to a whole new level

SLIPPER LIMPET

Sea snail · *Crepidula fornicata*

If you turn this shell upside-down you will see a small ledge and a deeper hollow – a bit like an old-fashioned house slipper, hence the common name.

So far, so relatively ordinary. But the slipper limpet leads an extraordinary life, starting out as a male snail, and at some point, if needed, changing sex to female.

Slipper limpets attach not just to rocks, but to each other. They live in 'stacks' that can be six snails high, and if a male lands on a limpet tower with no females below, it will slowly transition and become a female, in order to reproduce. The big ones at the bottom of the stack are the females, the smaller ones on top are male so where the snail finds itself in the pile detemines what sex it will be.

Look for cream or pink oval shells, often streaked with red or brown, and stacked in piles.

This is a small to medium-sized snail that can grow up to 5 cm (2 in).

The slipper limpet is an interloper on UK shores, having first hitched a ride across the Atlantic with a shipment of American oysters back in 1870.

These creatures may look static once piled high, but they can move, and will do so for a better position or to start a new stack.

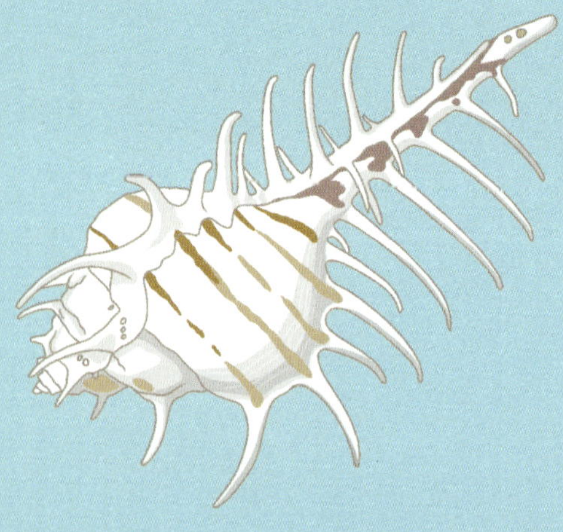

Prized for its dramatic sculpted exterior and internal beauty

SPINY MUREX

Large sea snail · *Poirieria zelandica*

This is not a creature to be messed with – the shell is a thing of great beauty and much prized among shell collectors – but this is a ferocious and unapologetic predator that drills holes in the shells of other molluscs in order to consume them.

The gorgeous spiny exterior is designed to act as a protective cage, and a deterrent to predators. These shells are heavy and come in a variety of colours, from rich brown to creams. The beautiful polished-looking interior appears to glow in colours ranging from soft orange to luscious cream.

Endemic to New Zealand and Tasmania, murex are found worldwide, especially in tropical seas and close to reefs. The shell can offer clues to where a specimen has been living: those who made a home in shallower waters have shorter spines than those living in deeper waters, and murex that lived in muddy substrates have more slender spines than those living on sand.

The spines are hollow and made from calcium carbonate. They are formed from the mantle which extends out in intervals to create hollow tubes; this then creates the shape to lay down the hard shell.

Fossil records for the spiny murex date back around 5 million years.

In the late 1970s, the spiny murex was featured on the New Zealand postage stamp.

Historically, the mucus from some murex species was used to make blue dyes reserved exclusively for the robes of high-ranking officials, including royalty!

Divers beware: some murex species are venomous.

A reminder of the passage of time

SUNDIAL SHELL

Sea snail · *Architectonica nobilis*

The Latin name for this shell – *Architectonica* – tells us, perhaps, what is most notable about this entry. Meaning, 'the architected one', the name refers to the precise spiral construction of this striking geometric shell.

Another carnivorous predator, the sundial glides slowly across the sea floor looking for soft-bodied prey, mainly flatworms and sea anemones. It will quickly withdraw into its shell when threatened, sealing the aperture with an operculum.

The spiral pattern we see on this shield-like shell is laid down in expanding layers as the snail grows. The oldest, and smallest whorl is at the top. Inside the shell, there is a single, cavernous space which is home to the snail for its lifetime.

This species prefers sandy or silty sea floors and so its shells usually appear after a storm, although because they are so delicate, they are often damaged by the elements.

The sundial can grow up to 7 cm (2¾ in) wide but will never be more 2 cm (¾ in) high, which gives it a distinctive, flattened disc-shape.

This snail moves thanks to a broad, pale foot which it extends and retracts to hunt across the sea floor.

Found along the southern US coastline, especially Florida and the Gulf of Mexico.

Fossil records of the sundial date back some 65 million years to the age of the dinosaurs.

Over 200 million years old and still finding ways to adapt to modern life

THORNY OYSTER

Marine bivalve mollusc · *Spondylus americanus*

You can spot thorny oysters attached to boats, docks and ironmongery, with shipwrecks a favourite haunt (although you would need to brave very deep seawaters to find them there). In some parts – particularly the Eastern Mediterranean – thorny oysters are now seen as an invasive species, due to their prolific attachments.

Despite the name, these are not true oysters but are, in fact, more closely related to scallops. They do share the oyster's preference for sticking together in groups and cementing their whole selves to rocks and other surfaces, rather than dangling by a thread as mussels do.

Unusually for a mollusc, the two shell halves are joined by a ball-and-socket joint, rather than a 'toothed' hinge. Just like a true oyster, the thorny oyster can produce pearls.

Italian fossil records date the thorny oyster back 235 million years.

These beautiful shells may be white, pink, orange, red or yellow.

Important to Mesoamerican and Andean Indigenous cultures, these oysters were traded and known as 'daughters of the sea.'

The embryos start out as free-swimming, microscopic larva – like spinning plankton – which then grow into what look like mini clams.

The crowning glory of any shell collection

TOPSHELLS

Sea snail · *Calliostoma* spp.

Topshells are small, spiral sea snails found on rocky shores in the UK and US. Though species vary from region to region, topshells all share a distinct conical form, like a miniature tower or crown.

In the UK, the painted topshell (*Calliostoma zizyphinum*) is a beautiful shell with marbled shades of yellow, brown, pink or purple – an often over-looked and unexpected gem in any shell collection.

If you're lucky enough to spot a live snail, you'll notice how clean the shell is. This is because this houseproud gastropod uses its foot to clean algae and other debris from its shell, having a good sweep-up every 12 hours or so. It then eats whatever has been covering its casing!

In the US, the blue topshell (*Calliostoma ligatum*) can be found on the Pacific coast from Alaska to California. This cone-shaped spiral shell can be blue, green, brown or purple. Growing up to 3 cm (1 in), it favours the shallow waters of rocky, intertidal zones.

These shells tend to be quite heavy for their size.

Topshells like a rocky shore covered in seaweed – you may find them in shallow waters or as deep as 300 m.

Topshells graze on microalgae and play a vital role in keeping rock pools healthy and clean.

Their operculum – the small disc used to seal the shell – is made from tough protein and helps keep the snail safe from predators, as well as stopping its body from drying out.

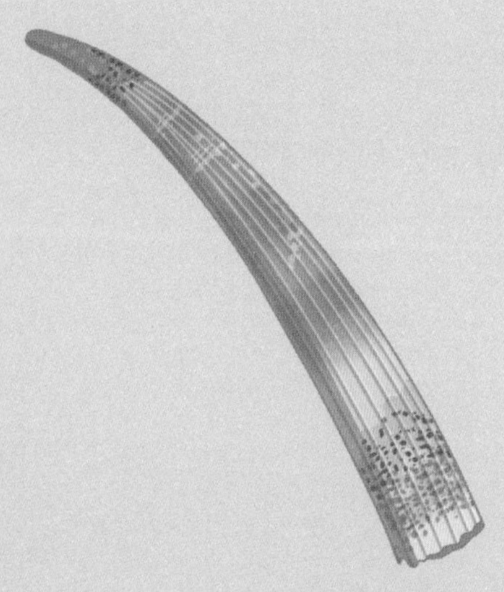

A buried treasure that rarely comes to light

TUSK SHELL

Marine mollusc · *Antalis vulgaris*

Long before mammals, there was a marine species that lived deep in the sediment of the seabed – molluscs. Fossil records show they lived around 500 million years ago!

Sometimes called 'tooth shells', the tusk, as the name suggests, looks a lot like a tiny elephant's tusk. The tubular casing, open at both ends, is a rare trait in a shell.

There are more than 350 different species of tusk shells and most live as deep as 4km (13,000 ft) under the surface of the water.

The tusk lives with its head – the wider part of the shell – pointed down. The tapered end sticks up above the sediment to allow for the exchange of waste and water. This mollusc has no gills or circulatory system and instead breathes across the whole length of its body.

Most common in the southwest of the UK and across the western Mediterranean.

Look for a small, tusk-shaped, tubular white shell with a pink apex or, alternatively, a yellow one with a black point.

Scaphopod **is the taxonomic class name for this shell. It is a Greek word meaning 'shovel-foot' which is the appendage the tusk uses to dig so far down.**

Tusk shells range in size from 0.5 to 1.8 cm (¼ to ¾ in) long.

The wondrous sculptress of the seashore

WENTLETRAP

Sea snail · *Epitonium scalare*

The name wentletrap comes from the Middle Dutch word *'wendeltrappe'* meaning spiral staircase, and that's exactly what these high-spired shells look like, thanks to the distinctive rib-like structures that spiral around each whorl.

You can also think of this patterning as a kind of ladder – each rib a tread – climbing from the base to the peak. Like tree rings, you can count the whorls to estimate the age of the animal who once lived in this sculptural home.

And while it is undeniably beautiful, the wentletrap is no mere ornament. It's also a lethal predator, especially if you are a sea anemone, which happens to be its favoured prey. The wentletrap uses a long, flexible proboscis (tongue) to pierce the anemone's soft flesh and to inject digestive enzymes, turning the victim into a soupy meal.

Historically, their rarity made these shells highly prized. Early scientific drawings described their structure with awe and reverence, calling them nothing short of 'wondrous'. In 1753, three wentletrap shells sold for more than £75 – a figure that was a small fortune in England at the time (about £25,000 today).

Most wentletraps are pure white, but some may carry a soft blush of pink or light tan.

They typically grow to about 2 cm (¾ in) in height, though larger specimens of 4 cm (1½ in) have been recorded.

Each rib marks a former edge of the snail's growing aperture.

Species occur globally, including the North Sea, British coastlines, Atlantic waters and along American coastlines, from New England down to the Gulf of Mexico.

A heavyweight with resilience

WHELK

Sea snail · *Buccinum undatum*

The whelk shell is likely to be the largest shell you find on the beaches of Northern Europe and North America. They've been around forever – fossil records from Texas date back 100 million years. So, while the whelk might not be the showiest shell, it has much to teach us about staying power.

One reason for the success of the whelk as a species is their wide habitat range – they can survive happily in shallow intertidal waters and in depths of over 100 metres.

Whelks lays their eggs in a spongy mass known as 'sea-washballs' or 'seashore grapes'. There can be up to 2000 eggs in any one of these papery, balloon-like structures, that you may spot washed ashore in a tangled mass.

The young whelks feed on their unhatched siblings for the first few months of life and then emerge from their protective balloon at about four months. It takes another three years to reach full maturity, and an adult whelk can live up to 10 years.

Long live a quiet resilience!

These shells are usually pale-cream to yellowish-brown, but look closely because you may unexpectedly spot a purple or green tinge.

Tough, local and tidal, you can find live whelks tucked under rocks or slowly crossing the sand.

There's something unmistakably British about the whelk – they prefer cold, oxygen-rich waters to anything tropical or exotic.

Most whelks now caught off British coastlines – about 10,000 tonnes a year – are shipped to Asia.

These storm-sitters are built for survival

ZEBRA ARK

Marine bivalve mollusc · *Arca zebra*

The alternating dark and light bands of this shell give these shells its name, depending on where it is found. Some know it as the zebra, and others, the wild turkey shell. This is because they look a lot like the tail feathers of a strutting turkey tom.

The shell is also said to resemble the biblical Noah's ark and, like the ark, this shell is designed to withstand the elements. These molluscs don't bury or hide – instead, they anchor to rocks, shells, coral rubble or the sea floor. And that takes a certain kind of hefty design – thick, ridged and immovable.

To stay attached, buffeted by tides and vulnerable to whatever else comes by, these creatures produce tough, silky and strong filaments (byssal threads) which they use to secure themselves to hard surfaces.

The zebra ark has another survival tool, too. It has a haemoglobin-rich blood supply which is rare among molluscs – this allows it to thrive in oxygen-poor and murky waters such as those found in marine harbours, areas which other molluscs would avoid.

Found from North Carolina to the West Indies, and especially along Caribbean shores.

These shells can grow up to 7.5 cm (3 in) long. The insides will be whitish or a pale mauve colour.

Zebra arks like to live in crowded colonies, weathering storms, silt and predators in the company of their own.

The whole intact shell is said to resemble the biblical Noah's ark.

With grateful thanks to publisher Kate Pollard, who first imagined this Nature series and invited me to write its shell volume; to illustrator Lucy Pollard, whose delicate, observant artwork brings these quiet miracles to life; and to designer Evi O and typesetter David Meikle, whose thoughtful craft has shaped these pages so beautifully.

My thanks also to our assistant editor Harriet Thornley, who has picked up the baton with this shell book and its companion volume on butterflies, continuing to champion this enchanting series with steady care and enthusiasm. It is a joy and a privilege to be part of this growing constellation of Curious Guide nature books, and of the team that brings them so vividly to life.

Susan E. Clark trained as a biologist and is now a nature writer and integrative psychotherapist. She writes about the quiet, regenerative intelligence of the natural world and how it shapes our well-being. She also hosts Curious Writers, a small creative community for people who want to explore their relationship with the living world and celebrate the often-overlooked wonders on their own doorsteps (curiouswriterscircle.beehiiv.com).

Quadrille, Penguin Random House UK, One Embassy Gardens,
8 Viaduct Gardens, London SW11 7BW

Quadrille Publishing Limited is part of the Penguin Random House
group of companies whose addresses can be found at
global.penguinrandomhouse.com

Published by Quadrille in 2026

www.penguin.co.uk

A CIP catalogue record for this book is available from the British Library

ISBN 978-1-83783-695-6
10 9 8 7 6 5 4 3 2 1

Managing Director, Publishing: Sarah Lavelle
Publishing Director: Kate Pollard
Project Editor: Harriet Thornley
Design: Evi-O.Studio
Illustration: Lucy Pollard
Typesetter: David Meikle
Copyeditor: Becky Alexander
Proofreader: Lesley Malkin
Production Controller: Sumayyah Waheed

Colour reproduction by p2d

Printed in China by RR Donnelley Asia Printing Solution Limited

The authorised representative in the EEA is Penguin Random House
Ireland, Morrison Cphambers, 32 Nassau Street, Dublin D02 YH68.